# Infant Baptism
## and the Christian Community

## Charles J. Keating

Twenty-Third Publications
P.O. Box 180
Mystic, CT 06355

Seventh printing—1986
Sixth printing—1985
Fifth printing—1983
Fourth printing—1982
Third printing—1981
Second printing—1980

©1977, 1972 by Twenty-Third Publications. No part of this book should be reproduced by any means without permission of the publisher. For such permission address Twenty-Third Publications, P.O. Box 180, Mystic, CT 06355.

Cover photo by Alan Oddie

Design by Maryann Read

Library of Congress Catalog Card Number 76-25620
ISBN 0-89622-022-2

# Contents

# Introduction

The day of Baptism is a day to celebrate! For our child, baptism is the "day the Lord has made," a day of new life and grace, a day of sharing in the life of Jesus, our Brother and our God. For parents, godparents and family, it is a day of pride, a day of pride and happiness for each other as well as for our new family member. For the Christian Community, it is a day of promise and of faith, a day to celebrate our Christian heritage. Infant Baptism is a celebration of our adult faith.

For that reason it is good for us to spend some time before the day of Baptism preparing for the celebration. We do that in many ways: by sending special invitations to close family friends, by making arrangements with our parish priest and by preparing for the family party following the Baptism. Because every Baptism is a celebration of our Christian faith, we also prepare for that special day by reviewing for ourselves what it means to be a Christian believer, a man or woman of faith. Ideally, we would all do this together in a few gatherings where we can discuss what we find in this book. Our parish priest would contribute to our reflections with his special knowledge of the Christian religion. This book is meant to be a discussion guide for such refresher classes in Christianity. The recently revised rite of Baptism calls for this kind of special preparation.

If we do not have such classes scheduled in our particular area, or if we cannot fit them into our schedule, we can read over this book reflectively and deepen our appreciation of those truths that we may have long taken for granted. The celebration of our child's Baptism then becomes an occasion for our own growth, a growth in understanding our faith and our appreciation of what it means to be a follower of Jesus of Nazareth.

Strange as it may seem, only now does the Roman Catholic Church have a special ceremony for the Baptism of children; up until 1970, the ceremony of Baptism was meant for adults, but used also for children! In the old ceremony, the child was treated as an adult, although we all knew that he or she could not understand what was happening. In this new ceremony, the child is recognized as a child. The responsibility for leading this child to a full commitment to Christ, to an age when he or she can accept personally the pledges made for him or her at Baptism, is placed upon the shoulders of the parents, godparents and the whole Christian community.

The Christian community into which a child is led by Baptism believes in a mysterious interdependence. We believe in original sin and in the Mystical Body of Christ. Both mysteries point to our interdependence: the good or evil we do is not ours alone; in some mysterious way our personal good or evil has an effect upon the whole community. We cannot hope to understand this network except in terms of crippled metaphors: the father whose shame or glory is carried by his family; the politician whose corruption or wisdom is attributed to his party. But we do believe that each unique member of this community, the Body of Christ, shares in and contributes to the health or weakness of the total community: "If one part is hurt, all parts hurt with it. If one part is given special honour, all parts enjoy it." (I Cor. 12:26)

**The** goal of our Christian community is to be visibly one, to be a united community in Christ so that all men and women might believe that Christ is the Son of God: " . . . that all may be one, even as thou, Father, in me and I in thee; that they also may be one in us, that the world may believe that thou hast sent me, . . . " (Jn. 17:21) One danger that threatens any community, and a threat, therefore to the Christian community, is the conflict nurtured by a difference between what **we say** we are and what **we do,** the conflict between our **stated** and our **real** values and norms. Our Christian community may say that its values are those of gospel service and witness; but the world is justifiably suspicious of such declarations when it **sees** our community as self serving, disunited or unloving. Service that is not perceived as service is not service at all. Our witness to unity is our service; it needs to be **real** and **visible.**

Infant Baptism is an event that challenges us to bring together our stated and real values and norms. We celebrate the richness of God's gift of grace, the divinely revealed truth that all men are interdependent, and that with the Baptism of this child, we commit ourselves to what we proclaim: a community whose visible oneness communicates that Christ is of the Father. The small child is a divinely created complex of appetites, potentialities and dynamics that need the proper environment to grow and blossom into the fullness of Christ. The immediate family plays its part in child's growth, but it will not be many years before this child looks beyond the family to the total Christian community; he will look with both hope and judgment. At his Baptism we resolve to meet his hope and judgment with the challenge to live his life so as to join us in maturity with Confirmation, and in brotherhood around the table of the Lord. It is an awesome mandate: to meet his challenge and to challenge him in turn. On the day of his Baptism we celebrate the excitement of this promise.

The seriousness of our promise brings us together now for this little course in Christianity. To refresh ourselves on who we are, to deepen our appreciation of all that God is doing for and with us and, to gain new insights into a faith that is ever new, are the reasons for our gathering.

Perhaps it would help if we tried to get a bird's eye view of what we shall be studying. In such a brief course, we have to pick and choose, and it is helpful to have some idea of why we have chosen to study this or that particular part of our faith rather than another part of it.

In the section "To be alive" we'll again reflect on some of the things we have said here in this Introduction, especially on our role as educators for our children. We can't get away from that task since our child will be influenced by what we say and do, even if we don't intend it. And much of what we say and do depends on how we picture God. It's very important that our picture of Jesus is the true one that we find in the Gospels and not one that we have dreamed up for ourselves.

This picture of Jesus begins to unfold in the second section of the booklet, "A Beginning," where Jesus' own baptism and its meaning for our Baptism is studied. The symbolism of "water" in the Bible helps us to understand something of Christ's baptism and our own; the change it makes in our whole life is studied. We shall be transformed as Jesus was until we have nothing left to return to the Father except our human life.

The change for which we are destined by Baptism is accomplished through the Word of God, the living understanding of the Lord in the Christian Community. In the second half of "A Beginning," we shall study the power and sweep of this Word of God in some detail. It will help us to understand why a reading of Sacred Scripture and preaching have been inserted into the baptismal ceremony.

"Action Today," our third section, is devoted to a reflection on the close relationship between Religion and Life. The Word of God that we find in the Bible grew up in Communities in which God dwells: Israel in the Old Testament and the Christian Community in the New Testament. The Bible explained the Community to itself, helped it to understand what God expected of it, and the Community then worshipped its Lord in the language of sign and symbol. And this, as we shall see, committed its members to live in a particular way, under a certain moral code of conduct.

The real motive for Christian morality is that we are members of the Body of Christ; our human experience is identified with Christ's human experience through our participation in the Sacraments. We are called to holiness because we are "other Christs," and, like Christ, our holiness will result from dying to our own will. Baptism is the beginning of this growth toward God.

"Free . . . at last!" (section four) reflects on the Christian code of morality and the formation of a Christian conscience. The Christian life is a joyous life because it is a free life: free to say "yes" to the Father and free from giving in to selfishness. Law has a place in our lives as we grow into mature Christians, but it is never enough for the Christian to obey the law; eventually, love should compel him to do more than the law, to go beyond the law. Only then will our transformation into a Christ-like personality begin to show signs of maturing! The final goal of the Christian Community that lives according to these norms of the Gospel is the transformation of the world and the restoration of all things in Christ. The salvation of our souls is part of this destiny.

The picture of the Christian that we shall construct will be a reflection of the picture of God as we find him revealed in Jesus. Once we have done this we shall discuss in some detail the new ceremony of Baptism, recalling many of the things we have already studied as they come to life in the baptismal ceremony. This we do in the section entitled "I . . . the Vine . . . You . . . the Branches."

At first we might feel overwhelmed when we look at all that we are expected to understand. If this is so, we should keep one thing in mind very clearly: Religion is not a series of facts or truths but a relationship with a Person, the Person of Jesus, and all that we study is meant to lead us into deeper intimacy with him. Our friendship with Jesus will be reflected in many of the things we say and do, in the choices we make and in the response we give to our children. The importance of our relationship to the Lord cannot be overemphasized when we are concerned about the spiritual growth of children in the family. No school, no formal classes in or outside of the home, can take the place of the normal family influence.

To help us find our way through these bits and pieces that are the highlights of our religion, there will be an introductory paragraph to each of the sections recalling what has been said here. Our study should be an exciting adventure since it is the study of our love. Let's begin.

Jeff Brass

# 1
# To Be Alive!

We only do well those things that we feel are worth doing at all. We have to know why we are asked to do anything. That's what this section of our study is all about: It will illustrate that whether we choose to be or not, we are the primary educators of our children. Religion is "caught" before it is "taught," so that our attitudes and reactions are more impressive to our children than anything we say—and our attitudes and reactions are influenced strongly by what we think of God. In this section, we'll reflect on our picture of God and on the need to look to Jesus for a genuine understanding of what and who God is.

"It's your **attitude** that has to change!" or "I don't like his (her) attitude!" How often have we all heard something like this? **Attitude,** the way we approach things, the spirit we carry around with us, can draw people to us or drive them away. Attitude is important. And attitude comes from our ideas and assumptions. We teach a lot by our attitude; we reveal a lot about ourselves. And no one picks that up better than a child!

A child, an infant, is like a sponge in many ways; he absorbs information without trying. The world is strange to him: it is large and he is small; it gives pleasure, but it can give pain too; it is caring and indifferent, light and dark, cold and hot. It is scary! The infant and young child wants to survive and be identified in this world. He wants to know who he is, what is expected of him and what he can expect of others. He learns much of this from what we do, from our attitudes; he learns a little from what we say. From our attitudes he learns about himself, about us and about the world. He learns about God that way too.

Our gathering together is to share ways that we can best communicate God to our child, this new member of our community. How can we share with him the meaning of Jesus in our lives and in today's world? We're not here to become theologians: we're not here so much to learn church history or dogma as we are to examine our own attitudes about Jesus. A child learns more from our attitudes than from what we preach. For him, it is what we are that counts, rather than what we say.

If we imagine God as an old man with a beard and if we think of Jesus as more God than man, for example, the practice of religion will have little to do with this life in the world, other than making it a bit uncomfortable with its rules and regulations, such as the Ten Commandments. We might even picture God as a kind of policeman or certified public accountant who is more interested in catching us doing wrong than in anything else. He takes the fun out of life. Unfortunately, many of us carry around such a picture of God and it shows in the way we act.

That is bad enough, but even worse is the fact that such a picture is contagious; our children catch it from us.

The truth is that this is not God's picture as revealed in Jesus. He said that we would know what God is like by watching the way Jesus acted: he cried over our suffering, he cured our sicknesses, he calmed our fears, he left us "Peace." For the follower of Christ, God is like that. For the Christian, God is a savior, someone who keeps us from hurting ourselves with our inclination to selfishness. He challenges us to love with unflagging faithfulness as he did, and he promises to help us to do it. For the person whose image of God matches the picture as painted by the life of Jesus, the world can be transformed through love. He is as much concerned about making the things of this world speak of God as he is about "saving his soul." Religion goes beyond the confines of the walls of the church.

Men have looked and worked for this kind of unity since the lesson of the Tower of Babel. That it is possible, that men could live in peace and communication, is taught by the experience of the first Pentecost when people of varying nations and languages understood in common. We want peace in our neighborhoods, where we can walk, work and play without fear; we want teamwork at our places of business. We want a single heart and mind in our family.

Man's search for peace and unity is so strong because we are made in the image of God, who, while being many, remains one: three distinct Persons yet one God!

This is what Jesus is all about. He entered our human history to show us how to live together in joy and in hope. He shall return one day to complete the work of reunion that he began, and is now continuing. Even now he remains as the Risen Lord of history to work through those who believe in him, so that through them the whole of creation will find union with its Maker. But the Christian awaits that day when the work of the Lord will be shown to all. For this, he works and loves and dreams.

# The Child's Response

There is no point is saying that you do not feel capable of communicating religious ideas to your child, or to the children in your family. By the very fact that a child sees you, you are communicating. So the question is not whether or not to teach; the question is **what** to teach. In a religious vein this will largely depend upon **in whom** you believe, even more than **what** you believe.

Psychologically, the child cannot help but adopt as his own the picture of God that we portray. Until the age of four or so, he is not able to think logically or with reason; reality for him is largely understood intuitively, grasped more by his imagination than by his reason. His hunger for self identity makes any message about himself or the world worth considering. He will readily take what is given, although he will often interpret it in his own way. It is this personal interpretation that makes him an individual, but it is his parents and family that offer the material for interpretation.

From the ages of four to ten or so the child begins to develop his reasoning powers, but in very naive fashion. His understanding of reality depends largely upon external authority and the environment, particularly in the areas of right and wrong.

The family, therefore, plays a large role, but not the only role, in helping the child form his picture of God. If God is "Father" in the child's mind, he will look to his own father to model what God is like. Where there is no father in the home, the child will have no immediate model, and might find it difficult to understand God as "Father." In this instance, we might compare God's never failing love to the enduring green of the evergreen, or to the love of the mother and other family members.

Because the child does not always remain in the family, he is also taught by the environment, the community outside of his home. Hence, the concern of the community on the day of Baptism. Through Baptism the Christian community commits itself to share with the child God's

Jeff Brass

own revealed picture of Himself in Jesus. First and foremost, this is a picture of love: "Anyone who fails to love can never have known God, because God is love." (1 Jn. 4:8) We offer this picture of God to our children by the way we live our lives. To live as a Christian requires the capacity to love. The task of the family and the community is to preserve both its own ability to love, and its children's capacity to love. It can be kindled, activated, crippled or destroyed. Such power we have over one another! Even more awesome, such power we have over our children!

Perhaps, then, the most valuable teaching that the family surrounding the child can give is to show him real love: giving of itself for the good of others. If the individual members of the family so live together, if they give of themselves for the genuine welfare of the child, his capacity to love will be kindled. If, on the other hand, the child's early experience is one of rejection, one where it becomes too painful to love because of the hurt rejection brings, his capacity to love will be crippled. He will become incapable of opening himself to others because he can no longer risk further rejection.

Such learning begins with birth. Psychiatrists tell us that personality is largely shaped by the experiences of the first few years. Of particular importance, then, is the physical and personal response of the mother to the child. At this stage of development, the child only understands through the senses. If he is to be disposed to love, he must be loved physically, accepted and appreciated for himself. Then, in time, he will find the love of God credible because he has experienced it through others.

The transfer to the love of God from experiencing love in a family is a natural one within the Christian family, a family whose image of God embraces the goodness of human love and of all creation. It is not so natural where one's concept of God leaves no room for the physical expression of human love. When religion is one thing and life is another, the child's image of God will be sufficiently distorted to require years of correction, if correction can ever be accomplished.

## Jesus Who?

Does it sound arrogant to say that one's image of God is accurate while another's is incorrect? Not if we believe that Jesus reveals God to us in the flesh. The picture of Jesus passed on to us by the early Christian community in the New Testament is the most accurate picture of God that has been given to the world. The living faith of the Christian community has preserved and developed this understanding of God through the centuries. Many of us have been exposed to this image in religion classes of one kind or another, yet we can always learn more about those we love. Especially, now that we are adults, our knowledge of religion, our image of God in Jesus, deserves to be adult also.

So, in the following chapters we shall briefly reflect on the Christian's view of human experience as an adult experience, asking ourselves what our baby, this new Christian, has a right to expect of us. What can we offer him from our understanding of Jesus that will give his life meaning?

Ed Curley

# 2

# A Beginning

Now that we have reflected on the importance of our understanding of God by looking at Jesus, we can go to the Gospels themselves. We shall discuss the baptism of Jesus by John the Baptist because it tells us so much about the kind of person Jesus is and about his task as the Christian Community understood it. Perhaps there is no single event in the Bible that tells us more about Jesus, the Father and the Spirit. At the same time, the baptism of Jesus throws a great deal of light on the meaning of our own Baptism. We'll reflect on the biblical sign of water insofar as it contributes to our understanding of Jesus and of the followers of Jesus; we'll penetrate the mystery of Baptism sufficiently to see that it touches our whole life. Of course, we could understand nothing of this unless we had the Word of God to teach us. This Word is not simply the written word of Scripture, but the totality of God's revelation to man, culminating in Jesus. It is a Word that is creative, illuminating and transforming, if we listen to it.

Beginnings are exciting, promising and sometimes difficult. All of us begin life the same way, at least physically. As North Americans we believe that we are all born equally endowed with certain rights and privileges by our Creator. But sameness and equality do not last long; the social and economic position of our families, our religion and our culture see to that. Soon after birth, we begin life in the mansion or the ghetto, as a Jew or a Christian, as an American with Irish ancestry or as a Canadian with French ancestry. And all of these differences, in one way or another, contribute to the richness of human experience on our continent.

Baptism is one possible beginning. It is one way of interpreting the meaning of human life. It speaks to the Christian of love, of cleansing and preservation, of liberation, of choice and of commitment. For the Christian believer, there is no other interpretation of human life that makes as much sense!

The roots of Baptism are deep, reaching back to the dawn of creation itself. In the opening verse of the Book of Genesis, we are told that the spirit of God hovered over the waters, waters from which all creation emerges. Although "spirit" here is the wind or breath or power of God, we Christians have traditionally understood the spirit in the sense of the Holy Spirit, the personified Love of the Father for the Son and of the Son for the Father. And we have seen our baptismal rebirth "through water and the spirit" (Jn. 3:5) as foreshadowed by creation itself. The Love of God fertilized the waters out of which all life emerged. So, for the Christian, the Spirit of Christ fertilizes the waters of Baptism from which the Christlife comes to us.

The waters of Baptism give New Life and destroy the old life of selfishness that St. Paul calls "the old man." (Col. 3:9) We share the life of Jesus as sons of God, joining with him as a New Adam in a New Creation.

Something of this symbolism can be seen in the story of Noah, where water preserves the good and destroys the evil. But our Christian ancestors saw the experience of Baptism to be even more closely allied with the death-resurrection of Jesus.

The idea of dying or departing from one way of life or one kind of life experience and resurrecting or entering another kind of development is not uniquely Christian. Many ancient tribes expected their young men on the threshold of manhood to go through some ceremony of dying to childhood and rising to the responsibilities of maturity. The enactment of a re-birth seems to have been fairly universal among cultures before Jesus chose to use it for the initiation of his followers: "Unless a man be born again of water and the Spirit, he cannot enter the kingdom of God." (Jn. 3:5)

The Christian community originally baptised by immersion, so that the candidate was totally submerged (buried) in water much like Christ was buried in the earth. In the baptistry of the parish church of the Holy Father in Rome, St. John Lateran, hot water pipes can be seen in the baptismal pool so that immersion could be carried out without too much discomfort. When the candidate came out of the water, he was seen to re-enact symbolically the resurrection of the Lord, sharing in the life of the Risen Lord as a son of God and committed to live in accordance with his new "being." So close is this identity between Christ and the new Christian that Paul could state: "Do you not know that your bodies are members of Christ?" (1 Cor. 6:15) For St. Paul and the early Christians, this was the basic norm for living a moral life: "Do you not know that your members are the temple of the Holy Spirit, who is in you, whom you have from God, and that you are not your own?" (1 Cor. 6:19)

With the eyes of faith, water is seen as a liberating force, making the Christian a free man: "You have been called to liberty, brethren; only do not use liberty as an occasion for sensuality, but by charity serve one another." (Gal. 5:13) The Exodus experience of Israel, God's Chosen Ones of the Old Testament, is accepted by the Christian community as preparatory to the liberating aspect of baptismal waters. Through the Red (Reed) Sea, the nation of Israel was led by God's power out of physical slavery in Egypt into their own nation. Water was accepted as the channel to freedom, God's instrument of liberation.

## The Baptism of Jesus

We all know that the baptism received by Christ at the hands of John the Baptist was not a sacrament (Lk. 3:21-4:13; Mk. 1:1-13). Yet, for our earliest Christian forebearers, no event (aside from his death-resurrection), seems to have been more important for their understanding of the mission of Jesus.

Principally, Christian tradition has seen the baptism of Jesus as a moment of decision on the part of Christ. As a true man Jesus was free, and in freedom he chose the role of the Suffering Servant, a savior who would face death and bear the punishments of others in order to reunite them with his Father. That he freely chooses to be the kind of savior his Father has asked him to be is indicated by the description given him: "You are my beloved Son, in you I am well pleased." (Mk. 1:11) This was a description hearkening back to the words of Isaiah describing the Suffering Servant who would take on himself the guilt of others while remaining innocent himself: "Here is my Servant whom I uphold, My chosen one with whom I am pleased, upon whom I have put my spirit." (Is. 42:1)

Adding to this identity between Jesus and the Suffering Servant, was the Spirit that hovered over him in the form of a dove. It also meant that Christ was the beginning of a New Creation which, like the first creation, was to be born out of water and the Spirit. Like the first Adam, Christ was soon tempted, but, unlike Adam, he triumphed; like Israel also, Christ finds temptation in the desert after having passed through water, but he triumphs where Israel fails.

But what does this past history have to do with us today? It tells us about the present. So profound and lengthy is our history as a Christian community that we can understand the present only in terms of the past. We are rooted **in** the past—but not **to** the past.

The use of water in the Scriptures, the lessons of the events described, help us to understand our own Baptism and the Baptism to which we shall soon bring a member of our family. Through Baptism we are given a challenge: to live a life without serious sin. In faith, we believe that such a challenge is fair because we can meet it living with the life of the Son of God.

While a baby cannot make a critical decision such as Jesus did at his baptism by John, he can be led to realize that such a decision is expected of him. Within the Christian family, he is gradually brought to the realization that only when he has freely chosen Christ, and his interpretation of human life, is he a Christian in the fuller sense of the word.

Freedom and commitment go together. We do not make a complete dedication of ourselves to anyone or to anything under compulsion; to choose in freedom is the only road to dedication. It is not unusual, then, that these are two major overtones of Christian Baptism. It is the role of the Christian Family to create an atmosphere in which the newly baptized can grow to make such a free choice.

# Infant Baptism

Although infant Baptism goes back to the time of the Apostles, it seems logical to question its value since an infant cannot make a lifetime commitment, nor even freely submit to the challenge the sacrament imposes. Perhaps the only answer to such a question lies in taking faith seriously. By faith, we believe that the infant shares in a new kind of life through Baptism: he lives with the life of the Son of God, sharing the Spirit of Christ through whom he can love the Father as a son. Such a share in life is a positive good that should not be easily set aside. In response to Hamlet's question of "To be or not to be," it is better to share the Spirit of Christ unknowingly than not at all. The situation is not unlike the share in human life the child receives through conception and birth; it is only in the future that he can use it to the fullest and give to all human living the fullest possible "yes."

For the Christian community there is no normal humanity other than that which God created in the image of his Son. We are truly human only when we share in some fashion the image and life of Jesus. Our Baptism, rather than adding anything unnecessary to our humanity, simply fulfills it as it was created. We shall see more of this in the following section, but mention of it here helps us to understand the normal acceptance of the infant into the Christian community.

Without his consent, he is accepted into the human community through birth. This is because life is good in itself. Without his consent, he is accepted into the Christian community through Baptism. In this instance, also, to share in the life of God's Son is a good in itself, completing the human nature given through human birth. The freedom to accept the challenge of Baptism, just as the freedom to accept life, remains intact. In each instance, acceptance is valuable only insofar as that life is lived in love.

Through infant Baptism, the community gives to a person the capacity to live a life free of the selfishness that inevitably closes one in upon oneself. Deliverance from such isolation is a necessity if we are to grow into a union with others that imitates the union that is God, and which alone can bring us genuine fulfillment.

Reasons for infant Baptism, therefore, are fundamentally reasons of faith, the faith that believes in the presence of a life that will only be evidenced in time—if we, the community, permit it . . . if we encourage it.


# The Word of God

The faith with which we encourage infant Baptism is a gift, created in us by God's Word. It is an increased capacity to accept all that God has told us about himself. And he speaks to us in many ways: in creation, in the Scriptures, in the Christ himself, in the sacraments, and in the community of believers that is the Church. All these ways may be called "The Word of God."

The Word of God is creative. Unlike our words, which can only encourage things to happen or which describe that which already has happened, God's Word **makes what it speaks.** If, therefore, a "happening" is an event that takes place without expectation and spontaneously, we might call creation a happening. God the Father freely, out of love for his Son, makes the world from nothing in a most unexpected way: by speaking! The very first chapter of Genesis tells us in its narrative fashion that God "said" let there be light, or dry land, or plants and they came to be.

For the Israelite, as well as for many current eastern cultures, the word was a sacred thing because it was a communication of one person to another. Even today in some eastern cultures when one speaks, one does nothing else; one's whole attention should be focused on this important action. The Israelite called the trees, the birds and the wind "dabar," (the "word" of God), because they saw nature as God's communication of himself. In the same way, they called the Sinai event or the Exodus a "dabar" since these were God's interventions into human history. "Word" was action and thing as well as a verbal expression.

When we speak of the proclamation of the Scriptures as "God's Word," we presume all that God's interventions into our history mean, and we attribute to that "Word," the power that it is said to have in revelation. The "Word" is irresistible to all things save man; man alone can close his ears to God's Word and be untouched by it.

It is God's Word that calls the Israelites to Mount Sinai and it is his Word that makes them one nation and his "special possession" (Ex. 19:5) by means of the covenant. In the Prophets such as Isaiah, Hosea, Amos, etc. the "Word of the Lord" constantly reminds the People of Israel of their covenant and recalls them to faithfulness. Gradually, the union between the Lord and his People grows into a marriage union (cf. Hosea 2:18) because of the Lord's relentless Word highlighted in the Exodus event.

# Jesus the Word

The final revelation of God is through his Word: Jesus: "God, who at various times in the past and in various different ways, spoke to our ancestors through the prophets, in our own times, the last days, has spoken to us through his Son, the Son whom he has appointed to inherit everything and through whom he made everything that is." (Heb. 1:1-2)

In the New Testament, Jesus is the One who "holds all things in unity," (Col. 1:17) in whom all things are to be re-established, (Eph. 1:10) and who will judge the world in the end. (Rev. 19:13) He is the Word of God made flesh. (Jn. 1:14)

In this biblical or poetic language, God tells us that he has "spoken" Jesus, saying in him all that God is, yet in a visible way that shares the full life of man, except for sin (Heb. 4:15).

The Scriptures, as they are preserved and taught in the faith understanding of the Church, are the norm of Christian belief and conduct precisely because they bring the Person and Message of Christ as Lord to us. They are the mirror into which we gaze for self-measurement, determining what is truly Christian and what is not. Yet, our faith is not in **things** or **doctrine** as such, but in the Person of Jesus, who alone is the fulfillment of God the Father's revelation of himself. Understood in this way, "Scripture" can be seen as the Word of God to which all Church teaching is subordinate. (cf. **Decree on Divine Revelation,** II Vatican, par. 10)

# The Church and The Word

But the Bible is not everyone's book. It is the family book of the Church, the Christian Community, who wrote it and consistently fostered its proper meaning through the centuries. It is like a family diary that has been kept in the family for generations and is best interpreted by the memory of the family as it now exists in the world.

The Church as the Body of Christ, made a community by its common possession of the Spirit of Christ, is the Word of God speaking to the world today. Guided by the Risen Lord who lives in her midst, she visibly speaks to the world of Christ. She does this always in subordination to the Sacred Scriptures, as she understands them.

This is the principal reason that the Church has added the Celebration of the Word of God to the new baptismal rite. Without the Scriptures and their proper understanding, Baptism could have no meaning for us; we would not know the why or wherefore of the Church. The new baptismal rite, therefore, offers a wide selection of Scripture texts that might be used in the service. A homily is, of course, expected for it is in full understanding of the Scriptures that the members of the Church come to a better understanding of our faith.

And this Word is meant to be creative, changing us and giving us new directions. It is the same Word that created the universe, molded the Jews into a nation and became Man in Christ. So our Scripture scholars are constantly working to improve our translations so that they become more meaningful to us; more and more emphasis today is being placed upon preaching and Scripture study for our priests.

Yet, we can close our ears to its meaning, as perhaps we have done in the past, changing little or not at all, as we listen to the Word of God Sunday after Sunday. The Word of God is meant to be a "two-edged sword" (Rev. 1:16), cutting to the quick in final judgment. We shall see later some of the striking passages suggested by the new rite of Baptism so that we might better understand its fuller meaning.

The introduction of a Celebration of the Word of God into the rite of Baptism also suggests that this rite is a community action, meant to take place within the community or at least with some representatives of the community present. Since the Bible is the Church's book, it is most authentically proclaimed in the midst of the community, and its meaning applied to the particular congregation by a bishop or priest whose special calling is to

Richard Bauer

preach the Word of God. (cf. **Decree on Ministry and Life of Priests,** II Vatican par. 4)

 Every effort has been made through the revision of the Mass rites to place new emphasis on the value of community prayer. These efforts are now being extended to the other rites of the Church. The Church, after all, is primarily a Community, exhibiting her authorship by mutual love among her members: "By this love you have for one another, everyone will know that you are my disciples." (Jn. 13:35) Only in showing ourselves as a loving community can we hope to convince the world of Christ: "Father, may they be one in us, as you are in me and I am in you, so that the world may believe it was you who sent me." (Jn. 17:21) In this united way we speak the Word of God to the world.

Louis Cremonie

# 3
# Action Today!

In the New Testament, the faith-event is the presence of the Risen Christ in the Christian Community. It is his presence that makes Sacraments means of grace for us; they are the actions of the Risen Christ in our midst. Through them, the identification of another Christ that we receive in Baptism becomes more and more profound until all of the high points of our human experience become united with the human experiences of Christ. In this way, Baptism touches our entire life.

While the Scriptures reveal something of God's interventions into human history, only in the faith-understanding of the Church are those interventions present realities. All of the events experienced by Israel coalesced into the one event that was Israel, a nation that witnessed to the One God—Yahweh.

In the last section, we discussed God's action upon us through his Word. In this section, we shall understand that his Word includes Baptism and all of the Sacraments.

Baptism, like each of the sacraments, is meant to consecrate a high point of human experience, to identify human birth with the incarnate birth of the Lord. Through Baptism, we begin to share in the Incarnation of the Second Person of the Blessed Trinity. And it affects the rest of our life. Baptism is not a past event, a once-in-a-lifetime event, but an event that touches the whole of our existence. As a result of Baptism, what I do—I do as a Christian, just as through human birth all that I do is as a human. It is so obvious that it is difficult to make a point of it! Yet, precisely because of the present reality of our Christian belief, we differ from those religions that spoke only of past memorials.

We have already reflected on God's revelation of himself through events. He reveals himself as Deliverer and Father at the Red Sea, as the One God on Mount Sinai and as the loving "husband" in the prophecies of Amos and Hosea. While the Prophets plumbed to the depths of these events, fascinated by their sparkling facets, it is still the event that is most meaningful to the Chosen People. No mere speech could impress them like the passage through the Red Sea or the Theophany on Mount Sinai.

Such a response makes the Israelites a Theocracy, a people in whose social life God plays a leading role. This People must never forget what God **has done** for them, for this alone marks them as unique. We might say, then, that there are not so much a number of events as there is a single EVENT THAT IS ISRAEL! They are a People whose whole existence speaks of God, so that if we speak of a "sacrament" as a sacred sign that speaks of God's action, we may say that Israel, in sacramental fashion, shows what God is.

This can explain the actions of this People who, after departing from God's Law by worshipping at pagan shrines or doubting his care, can return to him with the cry "save your own glory," or in battle threaten the Lord that for Israel to be beaten is for God himself to be beaten! (Deut. 1-11; Ps. 80 & 106; Joshua 24) Israel was the EVENT of God in the world.

The interventions of God in the history of Israel that made these people an EVENT were recalled in their public worship, centered about God's Presence in the Temple, but celebrated in the home at Passover time, or at the Feast of Tents or Yom Kippur. (Deut. 6:4 ff; Jer. 7) It is not surprising, therefore, that this constant and public reassurance of God's Covenant led to a sacred literature in which were written the great acts of God. In this way, the Old Testament was formed and the care of God for his People could be passed on from century to century with reasonable accuracy.

The Scriptures, therefore, besides being a recollection of past events that accounted for the present Assembly or action, became also a passing on of orthodox belief. So intimately were they associated with the liturgy that they became the liturgy extended. The People would gather together, have the Covenant read to them and have it explained, repeating their acceptance, as their ancestors had done at Sinai. When the Scriptures were recited at home they became an extension of the liturgy, which, at the same time, publicly dramatized the Scriptures. Still, what was celebrated was a **past** event.

# In Our Day

The main difference between the EVENT of Israel and the EVENT of the Christian Church is that the EVENT of the Church is an on-going, present EVENT. Although it is rooted in history, it is the reality of the Risen Lord in our midst today.

At the same time, there are great similarities between the Old and the New Testaments. Just as the Old Covenant found its expression in the assembled People, recalling and re-enacting the wonderful works of God, so the New Covenant found expression in the Eucharistic assembly. As the Old Testament Scriptures grew out of the assembly (gathering for worship) of the Israelites, so the New Testament Scriptures grew out of the assembly of the Christians. At the celebration of the Eucharist, the words of Christ were recalled and the letters from the Apostles and Paul were read and explained.

In the New Testament, however, the Scriptures and the liturgy combined to form God's revelation to man in a present event. This EVENT of the New Testament is the PRESENCE of Christ in his members and in the appearance of Bread and Wine. The ultimate goal of Christ's PRESENCE is the unity of all Christians, a unity to which all are called at the reception of Baptism.

Unity within the Church or, more especially, unity among all Christians whose loyalty is to different churches is, as we have already suggested, essential if the world is to believe that Jesus is sent by the Father. Both the sacraments of Baptism and Eucharist speak of this thrust toward unity in the language of sign and symbol: the oneness of Baptism itself, (the acceptance of doing what Jesus wanted done), and the one Bread and the one Cup that all are called to share.

The Scriptures and their explanation help to specify and identify this symbolic language. Because it is a language that speaks of a present reality, that the intervention of God in the life of his People is not something essentially past, the clarification that comes through the Word of God is always an explanation of what is occurring here and now.

For those taking part in a Baptism, this means that the candidate is entering the New Creation with a set of values contrary to the world's. He is sharing the life of the Son of God and he is becoming a member of the Body of Christ; he will contribute to its building up or its tearing down.

Yet, none of these aspects are clear in the liturgical action without enlightenment from the Scriptures and, therefore, without faith. For this reason, we often read that a Christian shares in the death-resurrection of the Lord through "faith and the **sacraments of faith!**" With faith and, therefore, in freedom, the Christian accepts the fact of his union with the Risen Lord, and interprets the whole of his life in terms of the death-resurrection of

Christ. Living the values of the New Creation, the Christian knows that he must forego many earthly values. Such heroism would seem to be possible only if we have the conviction of the presence of the Lord inspiring us **now,** advising us **now,** loving us **now.**

This means that life, liturgy and scripture are linked closely together. Even before the New Testament was actually written down, when it was preached and spoken verbally through liturgical actions, the Christian assembled, worshipped and lived out the message of Christ. Only later was it put into a book! In other words, the life of the community was the first explanation of the New Testament, so that the New Testament must be read first of all within the context of the Christian life. The faith-understanding of the Church still continues to clarify the Scriptures today just as Scripture continues to clarify the Church. But both Scripture and Sacraments are in the service of life, which alone is immortal, and will continue when there is no need of either Scripture or Sacraments.

# Change and The Christian

Because we are not yet what we are meant to become, change is part and parcel of being Christian. We are to be transformed, following in the footsteps of Christ who has gone before us. The purpose of sacraments is to consecrate and identify the high points of human experience so that they are transformed in and with Jesus the Lord.

In other words, religion for the Christian is the whole of his life; again, if we understand that "sacramental" means an outward sign of what is sacred but unseen, the life of the Christian is sacramental. It is a visible witnessing to Christ in the world. Sacraments give meaning and direction to our human experience in the sense that they explicitly point to the identification between our life and the life of Jesus. In this sense, they are but the more intense manifestation of what should form the fabric of all Christian life.

In the Sacraments, the Church incorporates the Christian into the life of Christ, so that each Christian lives in his own life the most intense transformation in the life of Christ: **the passage from death to life.** Lived more and more profoundly and consciously, the Christian life becomes holier, entering more intimately into a relationship with Jesus. The capacity to respond to this intimacy is grace.

But perhaps we think that Jesus never changed! If we thought that, we would be in error. Scripture and the Church have told us time and time again that Jesus was like us in every way except for sin during his earthly life. He left behind him all the qualities of his Divinity when he became man: "His state was divine, yet he did not cling to his equality with God but emptied himself to assume the condition of a slave, and became as men are; and being as all men are, he was humbled yet, even to accepting death, death on a cross." (Phil. 2:6-8) We know that this was not so of Jesus after his resurrection, since he passed through walls, appeared and disappeared equally suddenly. Jesus, after the resurrection, was not the same as he was before; through death he entered a truly human, but completely different life than we experience on this side of the grave.

Yet, while he was with us in our life-state he could live by faith, hope, fear, anxiety, and feel the tug of temptation. The mystery of the Incarnation lies precisely in the fact that he truly lived as one of us in complete authenticity, while being the Son of God. The reason for the Incarnation, as we shall see in detail shortly, was to be truly one of us without ever saying "no" to his Father. He came to live a life of love in a world of selfishness. The Second Vatican Council in its **Decree on Missionary Activity in the Church** (par. 3) reflects this teaching of the Church Fathers: "The sainted Fathers of the Church firmly proclaim that what was not taken up by Christ was not healed."

The transformation experienced by Christ through death-resurrection seems to have climaxed a life of transformation and searching. As mentioned previously,

Gordon Alexander

his baptism by John was a turning point in his life, a moment when he freely chose to be the Suffering Messiah to which he felt he was called. If we leave aside for a moment the strict interpretation of the Scripture scholars about the instance of Jesus teaching in the Temple at the age of twelve, we can imagine that this, also, was a turning point for Jesus. It is not unlikely that he thought his mission was to begin at the age at which he was officially a man, having gone through his Bar Mitzvah, until the effect his decision had on Mary and Joseph raised doubts in his mind. There seem to be indications that Jesus truly grew in an understanding of his vocation as most of us do. So change was natural to him—and to us.

   **The essence of sharing life with Jesus is to share his transformation.** Not every action in the life of Christ, however, is to be re-lived by the Christian. Certain actions are symbolic and we can identify with them; other actions are not. A child, for instance, may do many things: wash his face, make mud pies or eat his supper. If another child does the same things, we cannot say there is any connection between the two. Such actions are not symbolic as such. If, however, two children gave cards or presents to their mothers on Mother's Day, we could view such an action as symbolic and draw some identification between the two children. Both are fundamentally testifying to their relationship with mother, and this can be shared by others who have mothers.

Birth, growth, our relationships with others, death and our service to the Christian Community are likewise symbolic acts that have universal human significance . . . the high points of human experience. It is not unlikely that St. Thomas Aquinas had this in mind when he paralleled the seven sacraments with birth, nutrition, growth, marriage, healing, service to the Church and death.

As mentioned above, through Baptism we die to a world whose norm is selfishness, and rise to a new life where faithful love is the challenge. The world that we die to is not the good world of creation, but the world that has been distorted by man's selfishness—the world for which Jesus will pray. (Jn. 17:9) Because we are born into a part of that world that is without Christ, we find ourselves inexorably drawn to evil. We verge on a state of alienation from the Father because we do not share the life of his Son whose image we are meant to reflect. We are in a state of original sin.

The Christian believes that union with the Father is possible only through sharing the life of Christ and approaching the Father as a son. To do this, the Father and Son have promised to send us their Spirit, the Spirit of Love, if we believe in Jesus as the Christ. Working through the faith of the Christian Community which, as the Body of Christ makes Christ present, Jesus uses the instrument of water to bring the Christian to share in his own filial life. By sharing in this new life and already possessing human life, the Christian might be said to have his human birth identified with the birth of Jesus, and in this way he now shares in the Incarnation.

Henceforth, whether he is conscious of it or not, the newly-baptized cannot act except as a Christian, just as a man cannot act except as a man. He has been changed. Without faith and an exposure to the Scriptures this change will not be meaningful, either for salvation or damnation, since we shall be judged by our conscience. However, should the transformation be understood and accepted, the new Christian as he matures becomes a visible witness to all men, (as a member of the Christian community), that Christ still is working to transform the whole of creation. (Rom. 8:22-23)

Still, the new Christian has only been born and is spiritually a child. He has not been called to take upon himself the responsibilities of maturity. If he is to be transformed with Christ, however, he cannot avoid this: being a man for others. His human maturity cannot be left outside of his Christian existence! A child is not expected to contribute to the Community; rather he is dependent upon it. A grown-up is supposed to "pull his weight!" Maturity is a major human experience and it is identified with Christ's own experience of maturity when he acts upon us through the sacrament of Confirmation.

With Confirmation, human maturity being achieved to some extent, we are deputed to bring the message of Christ to others. Not all of us are expected to be preachers or teachers as such; but we are expected to live our lives in such a way that without Christ, they would be quite foolish. We are expected to become involved when others will not, to say "no" to the easy promotion that could be had by besmirching another, to worship when we have never had a religious experience. These modes of behavior, and many others that are Christian, seem foolish to the world but such conduct "preaches" the unity among men that Christ can bring. The mature man, he who is capable of loving the other without his own personal good being uppermost in his mind, has his maturity consecrated and identified with the maturity of Christ through Confirmation.

Another major aspect of the human condition is our association and relationship with other people. St. Thomas taught that the primary purpose of the Eucharist was to bring about the unity of the Body of Christ, since this is what the sharing of the one Bread and the one Cup signified. Our participation in the celebration of the Eucharist, therefore, identifies our relationship with others as a Christ-like relationship. As one spiritual writer puts it when he speaks of the reception of Holy Communion, "When we swallow Christ we swallow our brother as well."

At every Eucharist, those who have been called by the Father in Baptism are called into assembly to hear the Word of God, be changed by it, and to do what Christ did: to offer him in total filial obedience to the Father as a sacrifice of love. Jesus took the things of this world and in their midst showed unfailing love to his Father and to men. The Christian pledges himself to a like commitment with his celebration of every Eucharist. Celebrated with this realization, the Mass cannot help but change one's

Carl Pfeifer

relationship to others; once having entered into Eucharist I can never approach my brother except in love.

The Sacrament of Penance cannot, of course, consecrate the human experience of sin and forgiveness both because Christ never sinned, and because sin was not intended to be part of the human condition by the Creator; sin is of our own doing and it makes us less than human as God created us! But Penance can easily be appreciated as a "difficult Baptism" or a "second plank of salvation" to which we cling when the innocence of Baptism has been lost. Through Penance, we turn from within ourselves where sin has led us, and become open once more to the love of the Father in Christ. In its current communal setting, Penance is one of the most powerful signs of our interdependence, our power to heal or to wound the Body of Christ. In its healing strength, it speaks to us of the central mission of Christ, to preach the Good News that sin is forgiven. I shall have more to say about our understanding of Penance and Christian morality in the next section.

# Adult Christianity

Through Confirmation our maturity is identified with Christ's maturity. A specific aspect of maturity, however, is the service we render to the total community. We have already seen how God raised the union he felt with Israel to the level of a marriage union. We can recall how Jesus referred to himself as the bridegroom; we can also call to mind how St. Paul compares the union between a man and a woman in marriage to the union between Christ and his Church. (cf. Mk. 2:19; Eph. 5)

The love and affection between husband and wife should reveal to them something of the love and devotion between Christ and his People, the Church. Likewise, the oneness of mind and heart exhibited by the married to the Community should make the Community understand more deeply its union with the Lord. In this fashion, marriage serves the Community in sacramental fashion; it is not only for the husband and wife but, like Christ, it is also for others!

Holy Orders also fulfill the command of Christ that those who are responsible for the Community serve it. (Mt. 20:24-28) Any society needs those who will guide and teach, those leaders who discern the paths in keeping with its purpose and distinguish those paths from false roads. For Christ's Church, there is a need for those who will hold fast to the teaching of the Apostles as they have borne witness to Christ. There is a need for those who preside at the Eucharist when the Church is most truly herself, so that they might give direction to the assembly and apply the Word to the particular congregation that is present. In this fashion, the bishop, priest and deacon serve the Community and continue the work of Christ by identifying such service with His in the sacrament of Orders.

The Anointing of the Sick also consecrates a significant moment of human experience and identifies it with the human experience of the Lord. Every serious illness reminds us of the inevitability of our death; it is the harbinger of our final transformation into Christ. The Anointing takes that moment and identifies it with the healing ministry of Christ, Who conquered death. We are Anointed in serious illness to be healed, bodily and spiritually.

Viaticum is the Sacrament that unites our experience of death with the death experience of Jesus. If we allow Viaticum to have its full effect, our final significant human experience in this world becomes identified with the transforming experience of Christ's own death on the Cross. With Him we enter into our resurrection!

Through Baptism we enter a new world, a world whose values are found in the message of the Lord. We come into a world that believes this world is to be transformed so that Christ, the Lord of History, is "all in all." Once having been born again, the Christian lives his life with a consciousness of his maturity that has been consecrated through Confirmation. He should also have an awareness of his brothers that is enhanced by his celebration of the Eucharist. He shall pursue his life with the assurance that the love of the Father for him never fails, that the Father, through the sacraments, seeks to bring him into an ever deepening identification with His Son. It is our challenge, the challenge of the Christian community, to ever strengthen that assurance: by our own lives, we proclaim to each other and to our children that Christian life is joyous life!

Jeff Brass

# 4

# Free At Last!

We have to be willing to be transformed into Christ. In this section we shall discuss the moral response that is expected of "another Christ." Doctrine such as we have been studying, necessarily contains its own moral imperatives. The challenge is to grasp the doctrine accurately so that our response in faith and conduct will be genuinely Christian. If it is not, then Baptism initiates a distorted life of naturalism where we command God's favor by obedience to his law or a life of license where it matters only what we believe and not what we do. As usual, truth and virtue stand where balance is. Here we shall try to appreciate the motives for Christian conduct, the meaning of Christian freedom, the pitfalls of the "code moralist" for whom law is all-important and the proper formation of a Christian conscience. Finally, we shall allude briefly to the final purpose of the Church and of the Christian conduct of the individual follower of Christ: the transformation of the world to dispose it for the return of the Lord.

Christians are not notorious for being joyous. Smiling in church has often been frowned upon and "having a good time" is frequently suspect of immorality. We have rarely "lifted up our heads" as directed by the Bible with the conviction that our salvation is "at hand." So, why be Christian—why be miserable?

Well, if that is what Christianity really is, don't be! Fortunately, such a dour picture is a distortion of genuine Christianity. Certainly the struggle in which the Christian is engaged in a world whose values call Christ's values "foolish," makes the life of the Christian frequently difficult. But difficulty does not mean misery. We know that some of the most joyous people in our human history have been those whose life seemed to be without many comforts; we all know many "successful" people are alcoholics and psychotics. The problem is that we're sometimes not too happy as we try to give out of love; the purification of our motives can be painful and quite joyless.

So the joyless Christian is the dwarfed Christian. Somehow he "got stuck" along the way. To find the joy of being Christian is to take the great risk of losing all in the hope of a new life. This means fully dying to all of our desires as they are fashioned by the values of the world: success, prestige, power, etc. If we hold back anything, our joy cannot be full.

We come back, then, to the central truth that we must die in order to live. We must be transformed—like Jesus. We have already reflected on what this tranformation in Christ meant. **It was a trip to freedom, to be delivered from the limitations of the present kind of human life and enter a new life in which he could be always with those whom he loved wherever they might be.** It was a change in Jesus that allowed his Spirit, his Love for the Father, to be shared by all who believed in him. It is this conviction, that we share Christ's Spirit so that sin is no longer necessary for us, that causes Christian joy, even in the midst of our struggle. It is the knowledge that our acceptability and union with the Father lies in our sharing the life of Jesus, and not in our own conduct!

Our conduct, however, does reflect our share in the life of Christ. We act as we are: "Do you not know that your bodies are members of Christ?" (1 Cor. 6:15); "If you love me, keep my commandments." (Jn. 14:15) The "gospel" of the forgiveness of sin is a source of joy to us as long as we strive to act as God's sons. What Christ has done for us is allowed us to be here and now what we really are: sons of God. Before his coming, no man could live up to that title; now all who believe in him can! He is "savior," saving us from our inclinations to hatred, disunity and final destruction.

This is what we are constantly saying in our worship; it is the kind of life to which we are called by our belief. Just as Jesus symbolically took on himself the role of "Suffering Servant" at his baptism by John, and symbolically offered himself under the form of bread and wine at the last Supper, so in our worship we symbolically proclaim, in the language of sign and symbol, that we have died with Christ and are presently living a new life of resurrection. What Jesus did at the last Supper and what we do at the Eucharist, or in the language of water and word at Baptism, is real, although the reality is clothed in signs. But just as Jesus had to live as the "Suffering Servant," just as he had to mount Calvary in the language of flesh and blood, pain and agony, for his baptism and the events of the Last Supper to be meaningful, so **our worship commits us to live out in our lives of flesh and blood what we do symbolically but really in our worship.**

We worship as sons of God, and it is this belief that is the fundamental norm of moral conduct for the Christian. The demands of natural law, the safeguards afforded by human law, can only be scaffolding that supports our moral life until faith in our sonship blossoms into love strong enough to propel us beyond mere law.

If I take my own Baptism seriously, for instance, my life is already a resurrected life in which I have died to sins against my fellow man. The "empty promises" of Satan my parents renounced at my Baptism hold no attraction for me, if I decide to accede to my symbolic commitment. If I offer the Eucharist with full knowledge and understanding, I cannot be a racist, I must seriously question the possibility of a just war, and I cannot remain uninvolved in the issues of poverty and pollution. Through the Eucharist I profess myself one with my brother, since, only if I am with him, may I approach the table of the Lord. ("If you are bringing your offering to the altar and there remember that your brother has something against you, leave your offering there before the altar, go and be reconciled with your brother first, and then come back and present your offering.") (Mt. 5:23)

Therefore, what I do in worship and what I believe in faith, determine how I act as a Christian. Liturgy and doctrine have their own moral imperative. The remarkable thing about this connection, however, is not so much the relationship between liturgy and life or doctrine and life as the fact that I am free to act as I worship and as I believe: "When Christ freed us, he meant us to remain free. Stand firm, therefore, and do not submit again to the yoke of slavery. . . . if you look to the law to make you justified, then you have separated yourselves from Christ, and have fallen from grace." (Gal. 5:1 & 4)

By sharing in the Spirit of Christ, I am able to live a life free of serious sin. This was not so in the Old Testament when man was justified by obedience to a Law which, in reality, he could not obey. This is what Paul means when he says that if we say that our union with God comes from obedience to the Ten Commandments, then we are returning to the Old Testament and we deny that Christ has come. In the New Testament, we are not only able to obey the Law, but to go far beyond it. Our norm of morality is to love others more than we love ourselves, and no law could ever demand this since love must always be a freely given gift! Hence, in the New Testament, it is not a case of ignoring or denying the value of the Commandments. It is a case of saying that obedience to them is not enough for the Christian: "I give you a new commandment: love one another; just as I have loved you, you also must love one another. By this love you have for one another, everyone will know that you are my disciples." (Jn. 13:34)

# Code Morality

"If all this is true, then I'm not Christian myself. How can I ever hope to impart Christianity to children?" If this thought has crossed your mind, you have arrived at a major discovery about Christianity—that most of us are always "becoming Christians," trying to meet the challenge of the Gospels until the day of our death. Our task as parents, godparents, teachers, etc. is to help others in **"becoming Christians,"** and to share with them our dependence upon Christ as our one Mediator.

Long ago, there were some Christians who did not believe that our union with the Father was possible only through Jesus. They thought that if they kept all the laws and worked hard for heaven, that they could compel God to give them eternal happiness. They were called Pelagians and eventually the Church declared that they were very seriously wrong. Had not Jesus said: "No one can come to me unless he is drawn by the Father who sent me, . . . Not that anybody has seen the Father, except the one who comes from God: he has seen the Father."? (Jn. 6:44&46) We cannot find union with God except through Christ, he through whom the world was created and in whom the world strives to be re-established.

Today there are still some Christians who think that the way to holiness is through obedience to a law. By obeying, they feel that they have a claim upon God, and that their righteousness is a result of their own efforts. Some theologians have described this kind of morality as "code morality," meaning that for such Christians, goodness and badness are determined not so much by their inner convictions as by an external code of conduct. They attend Mass on Sunday, for instance, primarily because it is a law.

There is no doubt that all of us have to go through a stage in our lives that is ruled by code morality. Psychologically, we are not able to do otherwise, since we are not able to internalize our motives nor are we able to love in a mature way. Usually, we have passed through this level of development by the age of eleven or twelve. Up until that time, however, our conduct is largely determined by the reactions of others, reactions that supply us with a list of do's and don't's depending upon whether we are praised or punished. We are not ready to understand that some things are forbidden because they are evil; rather we understand they are evil for us because they are forbidden.

Ed Curley

Without such dependence upon authority, however, we would not arrive at that critical grasp of reality that allows us to internalize our convictions. With puberty this capacity becomes actualized, and we become aware of sin as the breaking of a relationship, instead of the breaking of a law. If obedience to the law has directed us toward fulfillment of our Christian humanity without wasting time in false directions, we are ready to do what the law commands for personal reasons with which we become closely identified. At this stage, the scaffolding may be slowly removed until our conduct is ruled from interior convictions and we are free to feel compulsion to go beyond the Commandments because we are becoming capable of mature love.

Until this point of maturity is reached, we also have difficulty appreciating the social dimension of sin. Code morality, dependent as it is upon external law, conceives of sin simply as a breaking of a law which involves the dereliction of the individual. While it is easy to see that the breaking of some laws, such as the law against murder or stealing, affect the total community, this is not clear in the case of every law. It is hard, for instance, to see the evil effect that evil thoughts might have upon the community.

Christian morality, on the other hand, rests upon revelation that tells us that all good or evil redounds in some fashion to the welfare or harm of the total community. This is the message of the Tower of Babel and of the division of the Kingdom of Israel—man sins and finds himself divided from God and from his fellow man. Our reconciliation, therefore, as illustrated by the penitential practices of the early Church and by the present use of the Penitential Act at the beginning of Mass, is not only with God but also with our brother. Only a morality that rests upon faith in the reality of the Community as the Body of Christ will accept such an insight. It is also necessary that one have a developed sense of community; like a critical grasp of reality this, too, comes only with the onset of puberty.

## Conscience Formation

We know that no one is born with a conscience, although many of us think of conscience as a "little man inside us telling us what to do." Conscience is a judgment and, therefore an action of the practical intellect, about a particular action here and now being good or bad for me. This, at least, is a general but accurate description of what the theologian calls "conscience." Much, then, depends upon my understanding of God and my grasp of his revelation, if my judgments are to be truly Christian.

Along with "code morality" goes a conscience that some have labelled the "super-ego" conscience. It is a judgment made on the basis of the image I have of my **ideal self;** a judgment measured by what I would like to think I am. Such a conscience is tyrannical, motivated more often than not by pride. I obey the law because I conceive of myself as a "good Catholic" or a "good citizen." As mentioned above, none of us can entirely escape this stage of development, but it should only be a stage. We suspect ourselves even when we are obedient, reflecting that while we are obeying the law, we would prefer not to do so. Somehow we always feel trapped with such a conscience, perhaps because we know that we are acting out of convictions that are not truly our own!

We are meant to go beyond this stage of conscience development. We are called to that freedom that allows us to do what we want to do because what we want is what the Father wants. But such a true Christian conscience, one that prompts us to go beyond the Commandments and allows us to act from our own convictions, is not formed at any particular moment. This type of conscience is being formed during our entire life.

As mentioned in the beginning of our discussions, much of our conduct depends upon our image of God, We are sensitive to good and to sin in proportion to our sensitivity to God. Our intimacy with God can grow, just as any relationship between persons can grow and deepen. I am sure that all of us have had such an experience of deepening understanding and intimacy with another, with a friend or husband or wife. It is a growth that is less determined by the things we know about a person than by our knowledge of the person himself.

So it is with us and God. We can learn a great deal about him from the Scriptures, as they are given to us by the Church. But only when we are attentive to the Spirit of Christ within us can we know him as a real person. If we reflect for a moment, we will agree that no one marries another because they know things **about** him. Persons marry only when they know each other as persons (hopefully). The fact that the girl or boy I love is short, blond, blue-eyed and smart is not the reason for my love. The reason for my love is that we have communicated, given something of ourselves to each other and found that which we shared to be loveable.

Revelation, as it is understood by the living faith-community that we call the Church, tells me things about God: that he is Father, Son and Spirit. We learn that the Father is a forgiving God, that the Son is obedient and loving, and that the Spirit allows all of us to share the love and obedience of Jesus. But only my sensitivity to the Spirit allows me to know God, Father, Son and Spirit in his intimate, personal life. In proportion to my sensitivity to the Spirit I become sensitive to his values.

Sin, we know, is a saying of "no" to God, a failing in the relationship of love. Sin, for the Christian, is not simply a breaking of a law, it is the rejection of a value that has been freely embraced through my intimacy with God.

The formation of conscience, therefore, is not simply a matter of teaching the Ten Commandments. As parents, godparents, friends or relatives of the child soon to be baptized, this will be only a preliminary step toward forming the conscience of the child given to your care or concern. He will grow in an intimacy with God that will impart personal values to him by the way he sees you responding to situations, by your reactions to him.

So, you will begin to distort his conscience if you become more disturbed over an accidental tearing of pants or dress than you do over his socking his little sister or lying about his brother. Such a distortion will lead him to lump together accidents and deliberate evil, the common denominator being how each disturbs adults (and to what degree each disturbs them). The result of this faulty teaching of values can be seen in those who still confess missing Mass on Sunday, even though they were in the hospital! With such distortion, sin always remains the fracturing of a law and not of a "relationship."

A true conscience can be formed only as the Christian is exposed to the saving acts of God throughout history and their meaning for us today. From the Scriptures, as understood by the Church, we gain an accurate picture of God and reflect on the response God expects from man. Such an understanding grows as the Community of faith lives out the Scriptures and deepens its own grasp of the person and message of Jesus as Lord.

# Conscience and The Church

If my sense of sin is in proportion to my sense of God, we might legitimately ask what right does the Church have to command my obedience. How does the Church play a role in forming my conscience? This is certainly a timely question today with all the discussion about abortion, birth control, etc.

First of all, the Church is a Faith-Community, a body that accepts Jesus as the Lord of history, God-Man, the beginning and the end that gives meaning to human life. The Church is a Community that believes the Risen Lord lives in it and guides it through the Presence of the Spirit. This Community does not speak of itself, nor does it determine its own structure and basic composition. This is done in the Scriptures. As a Faith-Community it speaks visibly and verbally of the message with which Scripture has entrusted it. In other words, the Church is not purely a human organization; essentially it is a divine mystery for it claims to be the Body of Christ till the end of the world.

The teaching Church, which helps to form my conscience, always speaks in subordination to Sacred Scripture as it reveals the Father in Christ, his Word: "This teaching office is not above the word of God, but serves it, teaching only what has been handed on, listening to it devoutly, guarding it scrupulously, and explaining it faithfully by divine commission and with the help of the Holy Spirit." (II Vatican, **Dogmatic Constitution on Divine Revelation,** art. 10) Church teaching, therefore, must always serve Divine Revelation of the Word of God; it is always judged by this Word.

Our conscience is formed by having an accurate picture of God, a picture true to what he has told us about himself in the Scriptures. The role of the believing Church is to assist me in acquiring this picture of God, Father, Son and Spirit.

Church teaching, therefore, is intended for my development of a deep, personal commitment to the Person of the Father in union with Christ as motivated by the Spirit. This is true whether that teaching be infallible or fallible, the principal difference being that I accept an infallible teaching in faith while I give only an obedient consent to fallible teachings with the understanding that such teachings may be changed in the future.

The Church has always maintained that conscience is the ultimate norm upon which we shall be judged. There is, therefore, nothing new in the manner in which we accept such fallible statements as those made on current questions of birth control and abortion. Our conscience can be in error, of course, so that any reservations that are made by an individual believer must be the result of prayerful consideration.

We Roman Catholics have traditionally attributed to the body of bishops the charism of discerning the true voice of the Spirit, so that we have never taken Church teaching lightly. While it must serve and be measured by the Word of God, more often than not, Church teaching derives from a grasp of the Scriptures seldom possessed by the individual. If we choose to digress from Church teaching on the basis that it is fallible, we should do so with the realization that we must stand before the Lord for our judgment.

Jeff Brass

# Moral Conduct and Earthly Fulfillment

The purpose of Christian morality is not simply to keep order and maintain peace. In fact, at times to be moral might mean to cause disorder and disturb the peace. So, by hindsight, we see that this is what the Church should have encouraged during the Nazi domination of Germany. In other words, sanctity is not always conformity!

Yet, surveys have indicated that many parents send their children to Catholic schools for the discipline inculcated there. For such parents, a Catholic education means training for "good citizenship," and the Catholic school is the big training ground of obedience.

The real purpose of Christian morality is much wider than this. Its goal is to transform the world. The power with which it seeks to do this is love.

God seeks to make a new heaven and a new earth: "Behold, I make all things new!" (Rev. 21:5) **Transforma-**

**tion and not destruction** is the termination of this world as seen by the Christian. We seek to establish the Kingdom, God-with-us, and we seek to do this by re-establishing all things in Christ in whom all things hold together. (cf. Eph. 1:10 and Co. 1:15)

The goal of the Christian is to imprint upon this world the image of God the Son, open in filial obedience to the Father, so that Christ might return to a world disposed to receive him.

We have seen little of this expected world except in the Resurrection of Christ. Like the Risen Lord, it is to be a world without the limitations and shortcomings that we take so much for granted . . . a world where love is more at home than selfishness, a world where there is total communication and understanding between men because there is total openness to the Lord. Baptism begins such a transformation, incorporating us into the Resurrected life of the Lord. Living according to Christian morality is simply the consequence of such an incorporation.

# 5

# I . . . The Vine
# You . . . The Branches

In the light of all that we have discussed up until this point, we shall now take up the actual ceremony of Baptism itself. There is little need for any preliminary remarks in this section but it might be helpful if we have in our mind the general outline of this baptismal rite:

1. The reception of the baptismal party and the brief greetings, ending with the child being signed with the Cross;
2. The Celebration of God's Word;
3. The Prayer of Exorcism and the anointing before Baptism;
4. The Celebration of the Sacrament;
5. The Conclusion of the Rite ending with a blessing.

All Christian worship is couched in the language of sign and symbol. Here (within the ceremony of Baptism proper) we shall find many of the things we have already discussed.

When the moment of Baptism arrives, as many of the Christian Community as possible should be present. In addition to the mother, father, brothers, sisters, relatives living near-by and godparents, some representatives of the parish should be encouraged to attend. It is a wonderful idea to have the celebration of the Sacrament of Baptism within the celebration of Mass at least occasionally, so that many of the parish community would be present!

Ideally, of course, Baptism is celebrated at the Easter Vigil or during the Easter Season, since this festal season focuses on the transformation upon which the new Christian enters with Baptism. Because this is not always possible, most Baptisms will take place on Sunday, the "Little Easter" that reminds us we have already begun to live the life of the new Kingdom.

If Baptism takes place within Mass, the reception of the children or converts and the Liturgy of the Word that is proper to the ceremony of Baptism, replace the Entrance Rite of the Mass and its own Liturgy of the Word. While the Scripture texts assigned to the Baptismal rite may be used, those proper to the Sunday will usually be proclaimed. In the distant past, the infant being baptized was given Holy Communion immediately after his Baptism to indicate that through Baptism he had entered the Christian Family and was welcome at the "family table" of the Altar. Although this practice was recognized as an abuse of the purpose of the Eucharist whose reception calls for some minimal understanding of the difference between ordinary bread and the Bread of Eucharist, it served well to point out the intimate relationship between Baptism and Eucharist. Even the present rite prays in anticipation of that day when the newly baptized will take his place at the Family Table: "In holy communion he will share the banquet of Christ's sacrifice, calling God his Father in the midst of the Church."

The present rite of Baptism makes it clear that the child should not be presented for Baptism unless the parents are prepared to profess the faith with some understanding and to bring the child up as a Christian. It may be, therefore, that while ordinarily the child is presented for Baptism within a few weeks after birth, in some countries a longer delay will ensue between birth and Baptism to allow for the instruction of the parents and godparents. Here in the United States such a program of instruction has been introduced in a few parts of the country. If there is any danger of death, of course, the child is baptized immediately with a short form of the ceremony. All of us have learned about this in school.

In the new rite of Baptism, parents have a much more important, prominent role than they had previously. It is the mother or the father, for instance, who holds the child rather than the godmother. The godparents, however, remain very important and their commitment to the Christian upbringing of the child is clearly pointed out in the ceremony; a commitment that was not explicitly expressed in the past. They should, then, be mature enough to undertake such a responsibility and have themselves received the sacraments of Baptism, Confirmation and Eucharist.

While at least one of the godparents must be a member of the Catholic Church, the other may be from a separated church or community. Unless that church is the Eastern Orthodox, however, the non-Catholic only "acts as a Christian witness" and is not accepted as a true godparent. The godparent is presumed to profess the faith of the Catholic Church in which the child is to be raised and the Eastern Orthodox is closest to us in this regard. Other Christians do not sufficiently share our belief to be committed to rear another in the Roman Catholic Faith. Godparents or witnesses should be chosen early enough so that they might attend the instructions preceding baptism with the parents. In this way, the day of Baptism will be most meaningful.

If one of the parents is not a member of the Catholic Church, he need not make the profession of faith asked of the parents and godparents immediately before the actual pouring of the baptismal water. The same is true for a non-Catholic who is acting as a Christian witness. It is only necessary that the non-Catholic parent request Baptism for his child and permit the child eventually to be instructed in the Catholic faith.

Parents and godparents together represent the Christian Community into which the child is about to be received. They speak for their own faith and profess to offer this faith to their new charge.

# Reception of the Child

There may be several children to be baptized on the same occasion. To simplify our discussion here, however, we shall speak of the Baptism of a single child. What is said, however, applies to the Baptism of several children as well with the minor exception that certain parts of the ceremony may be shared in by all at once, while other parts must be performed individually. If the number of children to be baptized is large, it is possible that other priests or deacons will assist the principal celebrant in such things as the anointings or even the actual Baptism.

The ceremony begins at the entrance of the church when the priest and his ministers, (should any be assisting him), greet the parents, godparents, and others bringing the child to be baptized. Unlike the old baptismal rite when the priest wore a purple stole for the first half of the ceremony, he now wears a "festive" color, (white, green, or red as the season might indicate).

After welcoming the party to the church, the priest asks what the name of the child is to be and what the Church is asked to do for the child. The parents may respond as they conceive of Baptism, saying that they ask Baptism for the child, or faith, the grace of Christ, entrance into the Church or eternal life. Any appropriate answer is correct. The priest then points out the seriousness of the obligation the parents are undertaking: "It will be your duty to bring him/her up to keep God's commandments as Christ taught us, by loving God and our neighbor."

Turning to the godparents the priest asks whether they, too, realize their responsibility to assist the parents in their undertaking. He then signs the child on the forehead, inviting the parents to do the same and then, possibly, the godparents. The sign of the cross is the symbol of Christ's victory over the selfishness into which each of us is born when we enter this world: Christ accepted death for having loved in a world where love was not at home; he then conquered that death when the Father raised him from the grave in approval of all that Jesus had done. For the Christian, then, the sign of the cross with which the new candidate for Baptism is signed indicates that this child is about to leave the world of selfishness and its values and live according to the values of the risen Christ in the Kingdom of God, in the New Creation. This the child can do because through death and resurrection the Spirit of Jesus was freed to be shared by all who would accept Jesus. The child will eventually have to commit himself to this acceptance of Jesus in order to be sensitive to the Spirit he receives at Baptism. But Baptism is the beginning of a new kind of human life for the child, a share in the only kind of human life that the Father intended—one that reflects his Son. All of this is said in the "sign of the cross!"

## The Celebration of God's Word

Once it is clear why the child has been brought to church and the priest has "claimed" the child for Christ our Savior by signing him with the sign of the cross, all are invited to listen to an explanation of what it means to be a Christian. We have already reflected on the importance of Sacred Scripture to answer this question; the baptismal party proceeds to a place where they may hear the Scriptures read and explained to them.

The parents of the child are free to choose any selection from Scripture that they feel is particularly appropriate or that has been a favorite for them. If there are many

Carl Pfeifer

Baptisms, of course, all should agree upon the Scripture selections, but since there could be as many as three readings there should be room for the desires of all to be met. It is important, of course, that the priest know well in advance what Scripture selections will be proclaimed so that he may prepare an appropriate homily.

It is necessary to have one Scripture reading, and that is to be from the Gospels. This could be a pleasant alternative under certain conditions, such as extreme heat or such, but ordinarily more than one reading will be requested.

To help parents (or even godparents) make a choice of Scripture, the ceremony itself offers several suggestions. These can be found in any Bible, so here and now we might simply reflect on the main points of each of the suggested selections. At the same time, we should remember that we are free to choose completely different portions of Scripture.

# Old Testament Readings:

**Exodus 17:3-7:** water is life-giving in the desert; it was the womb of life at creation and the means to a free life when the Jews passed through the Red Sea. Now water is given by God out of a rock, and St. Paul (I Cor. 10:4) will identify this rock as a foreshadowing of Christ and the life that he gives. New life is given to us through the waters of Baptism in which Christ acts upon us.

**Ezekiel 36:24-28:** through the prophet Ezekiel the Lord restates his covenant or agreement with his Chosen People. Spoken while the nation of Israel is in exile in Babylon, the prophecy assures them that the Lord will gather them together again and by pouring water upon them, give them a heart to serve him and each other, out of love rather than fear. The Lord's own spirit will be given them through this water.

**Ezekiel 47:1-9, 12:** in a vision, Ezekiel is taught about the life-giving power of water. All cities, all settlements are determined by the availability of water. The water that Ezekiel sees become a river of life has its source in the Temple, where the Chosen People believed that God lived. Through water, God gives life: a lesson in Ezekiel that is brought to fulfillment in the waters of Baptism.

# New Testament Readings:

**Romans 6:3-5:** a classic description by St. Paul of our belief that by receiving Baptism we share in Christ's death and resurrection so that we live now with his risen life and values.

**Romans 8:28-32:** Jesus said that we do not choose him but that he chooses us. In this passage, St. Paul emphasizes that we are called by God to enter the Christian family by God's free choice and not because of any good we do. God's gift of himself to us is a completely free gift that we cannot earn; we can only try to live up to it by having a profound trust in the Lord.

**I Corinthians 12:12-13:** through Baptism we become members of the one Body of Christ because we share the Spirit of Christ, his love for the Father as sons and daughters.

**Galatians 3:26-28:** the Christian sensitive to the Spirit of Christ, is destined to do freely what the Spirit prompts him to do; in this sense the Christian is a free man for whom rules and commandments can only be signposts to the complete giving of oneself that the love of God compels.

**Ephesians 4:1-6:** to be worthy of our call to Baptism, we are exhorted to live together in peace so that we might witness to the single Spirit of Christ which we possess in common.

**I Peter 2:4-5, 9-10:** through Baptism we become, like Christ, a living stone for the making of a spiritual house; we enter a chosen people, a people set part, a royal priesthood.

# Gospels:

**Matthew 22:35-40:** with Baptism we accept the values of the Kingdom of God which oppose the values of this world. Jesus summed up the values of the Kingdom in the two great commandments of love: love of God and love of neighbor.

**Matthew 28:18-20:** Jesus makes it clear that we are a missonary people, sent to preach him and to baptize "in the name of the Father and of the Son and of the Holy Spirit" as we now intend to do. He is always with us, the Risen Lord in the midst of the Christian Community that seeks to make him visible to all by its conduct.

**Mark 1:9-11:** we have already reflected on the meaning of Jesus' own baptism; he is the New Israel, the New Creation, the New Adam who has come to live as we have been made to live in a world that hates us to live so: that is, in love and without enemies.

**Mark 10:13-16:** Jesus tells us that only when we become like children can we enter the kingdom: dependent, vulnerable, generous and lacking deceit. We shall spend a lifetime growing into this kind of childhood!

**Mark 12:28b-34 (or 31):** Jesus proclaims the two great commandments as he is reported to have done in Matthew 22:35-40. In this description of Mark, however, it is pointed out that no sacrifice or religious act can dispense us from living a life of love; it is we who must be holy since things are not holy in Christianity.

**John 3:1-6:** Jesus explains to Nicodemus the importance of being "born again" through Baptism. We are "reborn" in the sense that we receive a share in the life of Christ through Baptism, just as we received a share in human life through our physical birth.

**John 4:5-14:** sharing in the life of the Son of God is like being revitalized with "living water" so that we never have need of seeking refreshment again. Jesus reveals this to the Samaritan woman, a woman who seems to have done nothing to merit such a revelation. So has he called us without any merit on our part.

**John 6:44-47:** we come to Christ only because the Father draws us; if we listen to Jesus and his message we shall hear the teaching of the Father. Eternal life, resurrection, is the goal of the Father's teaching. Through Baptism our ears are opened to listen in faith.

**John 7:37b-39a:** from Jesus himself comes true life; yet, just as Jesus is limited before his glorification, so is the Spirit. Only with the resurrection of Jesus is the Spirit freed to be wherever those who accept Jesus are: everywhere and at all times. Because Christ has died, risen and ascended, we are given his Spirit through the living waters of Baptism.

**John 9:1-7:** Jesus cures the blind man. This man was physically blind and Jesus cures him to indicate that he has come to conquer all the sickness that sin has introduced into our world. But we may also see a lesson of sensitivity to the Spirit of Jesus in this event. The man believes and is cured; we who believe can better see the message and meaning of Jesus.

**John 15:1-11:** we are very closely identified with Christ through Baptism. He says that he is the **vine,** the totality, and that we are the branches. He does not say that he is the trunk of the vine, in which case he would only be the source of our life. As the vine, Jesus is our life. We are called to conduct ourselves with a sense of being "other Christs."

**John 19:31-35:** from the side of Christ comes blood and water. The earliest of our Christian writers have interpreted the blood as symbolizing the death of the Passover Lamb whose blood saves the People from "death," and the water as symbolizing the new life that issues from the sacrifice of Jesus. Blood and water, then, were understood as pointing to Eucharist and Baptism which come from the side of Christ to constitute the Church, the new Eve from the side of the new Adam.

As is customary during the Liturgy of the Word, a meditative psalm may be chanted or said after the First Reading, reflecting on the message of the Scriptures, and an Alleluia verse may be chanted in preparation for the Gospel. The ceremony itself suggests portions of Psalm 22, Psalm 26 or Psalm 33 for the meditative response to the First Reading. These, however, need not be used if another psalm text seems more appropriate. The Alleluia verses suggested are John 3:16, 8:12, 14:5, Ephesians 4:5-6, II Timothy 1:10b or I Peter 2:9.*

A period of silence for private reflection should take place after the first of the readings, if there are more than one, and also, after the homily that follows the last of the readings. If the moment of silence, (allowing the message of the Scriptures to "sink in"), is not feasible at these times, it should at least be incorporated into the brief Litany that follows the General Intercessions.

We have already discussed how the homily should "open up" the message of the Scriptures and apply it to this particular congregation. In this instance, even if the Sunday Scriptures are used and Baptism is celebrated within the Mass, there should always be some mention of the mystery of the Sacrament of Baptism and the privileges and responsibilities that arise from it. The Risen Lord is truly made present in the promulgation of the Scriptures, directing and inspiring his People; the homily, therefore, should never be omitted.

Once having been exposed to a new facet of who we are as Christians and what our task is, we should be sensitive to the demands of love; at this point, therefore, it is suggested that we pray for the whole world. This we do in the General Intercessions.

At this point of the ceremony, we come to the first instance when several optional forms of prayer are made available to us. Our choice, as our choice of the Scripture readings, will be governed by our choice of theme on this occasion, our taste for this or that aspect of the Christian message, or even by our previous choice of Scripture reading. There are five forms offered to us in which we express our prayer for all men in the General Intercessions.

The first of these carries the theme of death-resurrection and Christ as the "Light of the World." It proclaims the holiness of life to which the Christian is called and prays that the new candidate, his family and friends may live up to this challenge.

The second formulary introduces the theme of the "royal priesthood" and "holy nation" into which the newly baptized will be received. Burial with Christ in Baptism and sharing, hopefully, in his glorious resurrection, are secondary themes that overflow into the petition that all the baptized may witness to the truth of Christ, but especially this new Christian and his family and godparents.

The third form of the General Intercessions recalls the unity of the People whom the new Christian joins; new members are "tender branches" of the "vine" that is Jesus. By our unity we are to proclaim the Good News of Salvation to all men.

The fourth formulation picks up the themes of the "royal priesthood" and "holy nation" again but emphasizes the role of the Spirit in the life of the Christian. It is the Spirit that will make the new life of Baptism known to our fellow men, that will prompt us to overcome selfishness and the "attractions of evil," and that will lead us to the two-fold love of God and man.

The last of the options focuses on the attainment of holiness in conjunction with our fellow Christians. We shall grow in holiness and wisdom by listening to our fellow Christians and following their example! We pray that all Christians be one in faith and in love.

The Celebration of God's Word concludes with a brief Litany of the Saints. In addition to the five petitions mentioned in the text other saints, such as the patron of the Baptismal candidate or of the parish or locality, may be invoked as well. The introduction of a series of invocations to the saints in Heaven at this moment reminds us that the Church, which we enter through Baptism, extends beyond the grave into eternity. We are bound to our brothers and sisters who have gone before us and we join them as well as our earthly brethren when we become one with Christ in Baptism. We pray that these brothers and sisters who have successfully completed their life may help us who are still on the way.

Carl Pfeifer

## Exorcism and Anointing

"Why on earth exorcise a **baby?** How could anyone think **he** has anything to do with the Devil?" In the old ceremony of Baptism we used to have three exorcisms and they have been the subject of most severe criticism, often phrased as above. First, the Church does not think the baby is possessed or in any way directly influenced by Satan or evil. But he is born into a world that only Jesus can save; we discussed previously how no one could live a life of total obedience to the Father before Jesus came. Jesus saves us from our compulsion to serious sin. But the child is not yet one with Jesus; he has not yet entered the "saved" Community.

The baby will grow and mature in a world where sin is at home and he cannot help but be touched by this world in his development. We have instances, for example, of children being reared by wolves and growing into manhood more like a wolf than a man. We cannot get away from our environment.

The child, born of Christian parents, is still a child of that world that is in the process of being redeemed but is not yet saved; he is open to all of the forces of selfishness and evil that make their home in that world. He cannot avoid succumbing to them, unless he begins to share the life of Jesus. So, now, in this vulnerable position, we of the saved community command that sin and selfishness will no more have power over him who will soon be another Christ. In this sense, we exorcise the baby, delivering him from the state of original sin into which he has been born; our declaration of exorcism will be fully effected through the waters of Baptism.

Two optional prayer formularies are given to us for the exorcism. The first of these points out that Jesus, by becoming man and living a life of total filial obedience to the Father, has overcome the power Satan once held over all the world. "We pray for these children: set them free from original sin, make them temples of your glory, and send your Holy Spirit to dwell within them."

The second form of exorcism speaks of Christ rescuing us from "slavery to sin" and the courage that this child will need to face the temptations of a world not yet fully redeemed. Finally, Christ's death-resurrection, his death blow to evil, is recalled to assure us that victory over evil, even in a world still struggling to be free, is possible.

The child may then be immediately prepared for the waters of Baptism by being anointed on the breast with the Oil of Catechumens. Where there is a large number of children to be baptized, or for other pastoral reasons, this anointing may be omitted in the United States. For the most part, however, it is an element of the ceremony that will be kept because of its profound significance.

Oil is a sign of three things: permanency, healing or strength and beauty. Here it is symbolic of all three. Oil poured even on a rock seems to leave a mark that is not erasable; the rock is changed forever! So, in this instance, the child will be marked forever as God's child through the waters in which he will soon be buried with Christ. He is not able to deny his divine sonship after his rebirth in Baptism any more than he can deny his human sonship after his physical birth. What happens in Baptism touches the child the rest of his life. He is permanently changed. He may reject his divine sonship just as he may reject his human affiliation with his family, but this does not change the reality of his relationships. He is son, human and divine, forever. Oil speaks of this permanent change.

But it also speaks of healing and beauty. The ancients used to use oil as a cosmetic, making one pleasing to another. As it anoints the child in Baptism, it speaks of his anticipated restoration to the image of the Son of God and the consequent love of the Father for him. Like Christ, he shall be the "beloved son."

Born as we are into a world where sin is more welcome than love, where to live according to the Gospel is to court persecution, it is not enough to know that we are "sons of God"; we need healing and strength to fight the battle that most certainly lies ahead of us. Baptism will not only present us permanently in beauty to the Father, bearing the image of his Son, but it will initiate the slow process of healing our weakness and strengthening us for the battle that every Christian must wage.

Oil speaks of healing to us if we remember the parable of the Good Samaritan who went to the unfortunate victim of the highway "pouring oil and wine" on his wounds. (Lk. 10:34) Wine was to sterilize and oil was to heal. So, in the rite of Baptism also, this first anointing speaks of the healing that comes through our union with Jesus. With him we shall gain the wholeness necessary to live as another Christ.

Even for the healthy, however, such a task cannot be accomplished without struggle. Oil anoints the baptismal candidate for this battle. Athletes used to be anointed before they entered into conflict, so that they were not so easily held by their opponent, and to give them strength. The Christian conceived of the person to be baptized as entering into a life of struggle like the athlete; the immersion in water was seen as an entering into the home of the evil Dragon and Leviathan, monsters of the underworld with whom Christ is conceived as doing battle in his death for our redemption. The immersion is symbolic of Christ's own burial in the earth where he fights to the victory of resurrection and the final defeat of all that sin and selfishness have inflicted upon us. Like Christ, the newly baptized is conceived as defeating evil forever and joining Christ in a life of resurrection. The battle of life most certainly remains (cf. 11 Cor. 10), for the norms of the Gospels are foolishness to the world, but the new Christian has been anointed, made one with Christ, the Messiah, for victory.

## The Celebration of the Sacrament

Leaving the place of the Celebration of God's Word, all proceed to the baptistry. The ceremonial suggests that this procession, as well as the one to the place of the Liturgy of the Word and the final procession for the rite of conclusion, be accompanied by song. This is another indication of the **community character of the celebration** as envisaged by the rite itself.

At the baptistry, the celebrant reminds the congregation of God's use of water throughout the history of his saving interventions into our human experience. Although we have already reflected on the biblical use of water and its meaning for us today, we might now spend a moment on the concept of "living water." The ritual for Baptism has traditionally directed that the waters used for Baptism be flowing, even if this could be done only by the pouring of the water. We can understand how water that is moving, such as in a stream or in a waterfall, speaks of freshness and life while stagnant water symbolizes corruption and death.

In the conferral of Baptism, new life is given and our mind recalls the waters of creation in which the first life was made by God. We can imagine the life-giving symbolism of water for the desert nomad, such as our ancestors. Ideally, then, baptismal fonts should be built to accommodate "living water" that flows. The new rite of Baptism reflects this presumption about the use of "living water" by encouraging the blessing of the water anew at each occasion for the conferral of the Sacrament outside of Eastertime, when the water has been blessed solemnly at the Easter Vigil.

Any one of three optional formularies may be used to bless the water. As was the case with the optional forms of prayer already discussed, each of these formularies has a particular emphasis, or opens up a particular insight into the mystery of Baptism.

The first of the optional blessings recites the history of water as the source of life in the Bible, recalling its key role in the story of creation, in the story of Noah, the Red Sea event, the baptism of Jesus, the issue of water from his side on Calvary, and now its role in the sacrament of Baptism.

The second prayer formula calls for more participation from the congregation, assigning them a response to

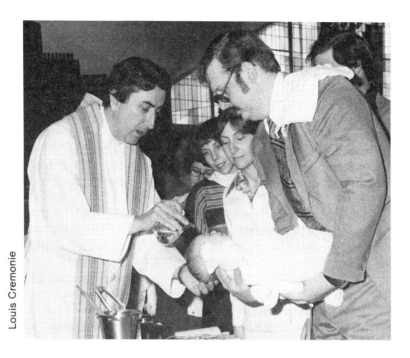

Louis Cremonie

each of the major statements of the celebrant. References are made to the meaning of water in the New Testament at the Jordan and on Calvary and the principal role of the Spirit in re-birth is outlined.

The third of the optional types of prayers for blessing the water spotlights the community formed through Baptism, a Community of faith and love whose purpose is "to announce the Good News of Jesus Christ to people everywhere."

During the Easter season, the water is not blessed as such, but parts of the prayer of blessing are kept to express thanksgiving and petition somewhere within the Celebration of the Sacrament itself.

Baptism is a moment of commitment; for the child it is his destiny to ratify this commitment, to accept willingly the new life of Christ with which he has been endowed. He cannot do this, of course, until he becomes sufficiently developed and attains that true freedom that makes choice meaningful.

In the old rite of Baptism, a rite that was never written for the Baptism of children, the child was directly addressed, and asked about his renunciation of Satan and his profession of Christ; the godparents responded for him. But this did not reflect the reality; none of us can commit another to Christ since such a commitment is a gift of love and must be personally given. In the new rite, parents and godparents are addressed, asked to renew and ratify their own rejection of evil and acceptance of Jesus. In this fashion the decisive character of the baptismal act is clarified and the reality of the situation is more accurately reflected.

At the conclusion of the questioning and the re-commitment of the parents and godparents, the celebrant joyously proclaims: "This is our faith. This is the faith of the Church. We are proud to profess it, in Christ Jesus our Lord." Should the group so desire, the entire profession may be concluded with an appropriate hymn, such as the song, **Profession of Faith** or **Faith of Our Fathers.**

The moment of Baptism has now arrived. Ideally, the child would be immersed in water three times, the celebrant placing the child in the water and the mother or father lifting him out of it. In this way the symbolism of burial with Christ is more obvious. More often than not, however, the child will probably have water poured upon him three times in the custom with which we are familiar. In this case the mother or father holds the child. Previously this was the responsibility of the godmother, and if circumstances so indicate she or the godfather might still fulfill it. Usually, however, the parent will be given the privilege because the first responsibility for introducing the child to the Lord Jesus is his.

In obedience to the Lord's command, the celebrant says "(name of the child), I baptize you in the name of the Father, and of the Son, and of the Holy Spirit" as the three-fold immersion or pouring takes place. Before he does so, however, he assures himself of the desire of the parents and godparents: "Is it your will that (name of the child) should be baptized in the faith of the Church, which we have all professed with you?"

Following each baptism all are invited to acclaim their joy over the reception of another member into the Body of Christ with a short expression of welcome. This acclamation is not unlike the words of the congregation following the consecration at the celebration of the Eucharist which indicate its faith and agreement with all that the celebrant is doing. Texts for this acclamation can be found in any participation booklet, but we are not limited only to the texts offered. A short hymn may also be sung. A sample of such an acclamation that may be said, (if it is not sung), is "Holy Church of God stretch out your hand and welcome your children newborn of water and of the Spirit of God."

Still at the baptistry, three (or possibly four) actions bring the Celebration of the Sacrament to an end. The first of these is an anointing with oil, the oil of chrism, having a meaning distinct from the first anointing. In ancient days priests and kings were anointed, symbolizing the permanency and richness of their calling. The prophet did not go through a formal anointing with oil, but his calling was seen as a consecration (cf. Jer. 1:5). Through Baptism, the new Christian has become another Christ, the Messiah, the one anointed and called by the Father as Priest, King and Prophet. The new Christian is to take on the task of Christ in the world.

As "priest," the new Christian shares in the life of Jesus who is the God-Man, the perfect mediator between the Father and mankind. With Christ, sharing in the task of the Spirit-filled Community that is the Church, the neophyte will one day stand about the Family Table of the altar and in union with Christ offer himself and the things of this world to the Father in union with Christ. The Father will share Christ under the form of Bread and Wine with him and the exercise of Priesthood, joining earth to heaven, will be fulfilled.

As "king" the new Catholic shares the rule of Christ over the words: "All authority in heaven and on earth has been given to me." (Mt. 28:18) The child will grow to challenge successfully the values of the world, if he re-

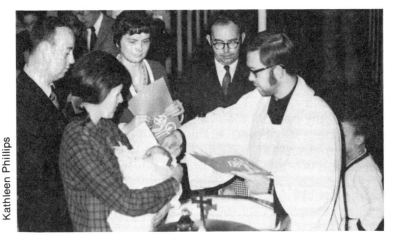

Kathleen Phillips

sponds to the Spirit of Christ he has received in Baptism. In this fashion he will exercise the Kingship of Christ.

By "prophet" we do not mean necessarily one who foretells the future. The word comes from two greek words meaning "to speak for another." A Christian prophet speaks for God, living a life in such a way that it would be foolishness if God had not spoken to us in Jesus. Hence, the gift of "prophecy" is the gift of "witness"; once having learned about ourselves and about God from Jesus, we carry this message in our conduct and word through life.

The anointing with chrism, then, carries with it our conviction that the child has become, in fact, and is to grow into another Christ, Priest, King and Prophet. Like the priests, kings and prophets of old, he is anointed on the top of the head, consecrated to the Lord for a lifetime of service!

In the earliest days of the Church, all Baptisms of adults took place on the vigils of Easter or Pentecost. The newly baptized were then given white robes which they wore for a week during which they returned to the community gathering each day for further instructions in the mysteries of Christianity. The white robe symbolized their new found dignity as priests, kings and prophets with the Lord.

The child is now clothed with a white garment, the "outward sign" of his Christian dignity which he is to strive to wear unstained throughout life. Ideally, this white robe is provided by the family of the child, but it would not be improper if women of the parish made it for the family. In this way, the community dimension of the event would be evident. There is no set form that the garment should take and much would no doubt depend upon whether the child is baptized by immersion or pouring. Baptism by immersion would find a fuller, more realistic robe much more useful than a simple apron affair which would be suitable in those instances when Baptism is given by pouring of water.

Anointed and clothed with a new robe of innocence, the child receives a lighted candle. Someone from his family lights it from the Easter candle, (which was blessed at the Easter vigil as symbolic of Christ, the Light of the world). As another Christ, the child shares in the task of Christ to be a light of the world; from Christ, he takes this light and makes it his own as he reflects the Lord through his own unique personality. At first, the parents and godparents will be responsible for keeping the light of Christ burning for the child. But, eventually, he himself must "keep the flame of faith alive in his heart."

Faith is nourished by listening to the Scriptures with attention and by speaking of things worthy of another Christ. Should the celebrant wish, he may add a short ceremony here to teach the importance of being sensitive to the message of Christ and speaking with wisdom. In the Gospels, we find Jesus making "the deaf to hear and the dumb to speak" simply by touching their ears and mouth while saying "ephphetha" (be opened). So now the celebrant may touch the ears and mouth of the new Christian while praying "May (the Lord Jesus) soon touch your ears to receive his word, and your mouth to proclaim his faith, to the praise and glory of God the Father." The neophyte is expected to grow sensitive to the Scriptures and courageous in the profession of his faith.

# Conclusion of the Rite

Unless the Celebration of the Sacrament took place in the sanctuary, (as it might, for example, if celebrated within Mass), there is a final procession now from the baptistry to the sanctuary where the rite concludes.

As all stand in front of the altar, the celebrant reminds them that Baptism is but the first step in Christian initiation (there remain Confirmation and Eucharist). To anticipate the fullness of participation in the Eucharist, all pray the Our Father. Traditionally, dating from the earliest of our descriptions of the Mass celebration, the Lord's Prayer has been closely associated with the Eucharist, being said in preparation for the reception of Holy Communion. Because it has also been traditionally prayed in the ceremony of Baptism, its use tends to bind together the beginning and the end of our initiation into the Family of Jesus whose Father is God. For us it is a prayer of yearning for that day when the new Christian will take his place with the Family around the altar.

The entire rite concludes with a solemn blessing. Four different forms of this blessing may be found in the ritual, but whichever one is chosen it is meant to replace that custom commonly called "The Churching of Women." This custom has carried with it the undesirable significance that a woman needed purification after childbirth. Such a connotation will, hopefully, not be attached to this new blessing. As in the new nuptial blessing, the father is included in this closing petition for God's favor and, in fact, so is the whole congregation.

Of the four forms, the first and the third are quite similar, asking God's blessing first upon the mother(s), then upon the father(s) and finally upon all present. The second of the formularies begs God's favor first upon the newly baptized, then upon both parents together and, finally, upon the congregation. The last of the suggested forms blesses all together without distinguishing between family and congregation. This last form might be useful where there is some embarrassment over family relationships or where sadness still lingers over the dissolution of a family through the loss of a mother or father. While it is certainly fitting to have some celebration at home after the ceremony, it seems that it should be a celebration worthy of so great an event. Just the fact that members of a family are gathered together is worthy of celebration, and it would seem inappropriate to have each go his separate way when such gatherings are so rare in our days of speed and business. From what has been said already, it seems clear that no one should be deprived of participating in the Baptism simply to prepare for the party at home. All should attend the ceremony and arrange to work together to prepare those last-minute "goodies" when they get home. The godparents could be of immense help in this way.

# 6

# Conclusion

And so, another Christian begins the Way of Jesus. If he is successful, the Body of Christ will grow so much stronger; if he fails, the Body will become that much weaker. We have spent this little time together to learn how we might do our part in assuring success.

Much goes into the making of an individual; in some fashion we are all to be praised or blamed for the success or failure of our neighbor—although we may not fully understand this mystery of human relationships until it is revealed to us in the resurrection. My openness to another, my capacity to love, to dream with another, to hope and to cry with another, all contribute to my growth and his growth. Insofar as I am less human, mankind is less human.

But half of my humanity is understanding the God in whose image I have been made. Righteousness and judgment will pervade my being, if I consider this God as the God of thunderbolts and retribution; apathetic indifference will characterize me, if he is a kindly grandfather; fear and paralysis will be mine if he is my certified public accountant who glories in finding me doing wrong; retaliation and rejection will dominate me, if I conceive of him as the commanding God who has allowed me to suffer unjustly.

Having completed our discussions together, we might question whether our God is the God of Jesus Christ, the God of revelation. Little can be done in a few hours, but much can be done in a few minutes each day, if we read the Gospels thoughtfully and with a willingness to change—if we have to.

And we all must change if we are Christian; transformation is part and parcel of our way of life. Our conscience develops, the breadth of our understanding broadens under the action of Love itself and we gradually become that which we have always been since our Baptism . . . another Christ.

Precisely because I am another Christ I know the Father as he is, as only a son can know his Father: the Father who is just in his mercy, who can love intimately and personally each of us whom he has made into the image of his Son. My love of such a Father is filial, patient, tolerant of my own pursuing incapacity, and trusting without being presumptuous. Such a Father and such a love I seek to pass on to this child whose life I shall influence in one fashion or another.

My influence shall be with this child all of his life, but perhaps it shall be the greatest when I am the least capable of knowing what I should do. The days of infancy and childhood are the tender growths that shape all the future—yet, those are the days when my child will learn more from what I do than what I say. And what I do is determined by the way I think.

Such might be my meditation as I come to the close of another opportunity to "learn of the Lord." We have reflected on the essential meaning of being a Christian in the Roman Catholic Church. Only basic fundamentals have been recalled, because basic fundamentals are so often lost in the details and richness of our historical developments. This is not to say that what has not entered into our discussion is unimportant; it simply means that it is not appropriate material for a brief study of Baptism, or that it is of lesser importance for a bird's-eye view of the Christian message. Even that which is secondary enriches our understanding of the Lord, as long as we recognize that it is secondary in importance!

Because the Lord constantly speaks to us in our human experience and we can grow in our love and understanding of him as we progess in Christian living each year, we cannot even now be satisfied with our own knowledge and picture of God. Restlessness is integral to being Christian. We should always be aware of our need to grow and mature, our need to correct and complete, our need never to be the same as we are transformed into the fullness of Christ. Few of us can ever say with St. Paul "It is no longer I that live, but Christ lives in me." (Gal. 2:20)

Yet, such a goal is possible. It is possible to grow into such intimacy with the Lord that our prayer is only his prayer; our love, his love; and our transformation into him complete, yet never so consuming as to absorb our own personality.

To this grand destiny the Christian is called in his Baptism. We have come together to encourage each other and to assure a new Christian that such a destiny is within his grasp as another Christ.